November/Noviembre

By/Por Robyn Brode

Reading Consultant/Consultora de lectura: Linda Cornwell,
Literacy Connections Consulting/consultora de lectoescritura

WEEKLY READER®
PUBLISHING

ROCKFORD PUBLIC LIBRARY

Please visit our web site at **www.garethstevens.com**.
For a free catalog describing our list of high-quality books, call 1-800-542-2595 (USA)
or 1-800-387-3178 (Canada). Our fax: 1-877-542-2596

Library of Congress Cataloging-in-Publication Data
Brode, Robyn.
    [November. Spanish & English]
    November / by Robyn Brode ; reading consultant, Linda Cornwell — Noviembre /
    por Robyn Brode ; consultora de lectura, Linda Cornwell.
       p. cm. — (Months of the year — Meses del año)
    English and Spanish in parallel text.
    Includes bibliographical references and index.
    ISBN-10: 1-4339-1939-7   ISBN-13: 978-1-4339-1939-8 (lib. bdg.)
    ISBN-10: 1-4339-2116-2   ISBN-13: 978-1-4339-2116-2 (softcover)
    1. November—Juvenile literature.   2. Holidays—United States—Juvenile literature.
I. Cornwell, Linda. II. Title. III. Title: Noviembre.
GT4803.B769418   2010
394.264—dc22   2009013990

This edition first published in 2010 by
Weekly Reader® Books
An Imprint of Gareth Stevens Publishing
1 Reader's Digest Road
Pleasantville, NY 10570-7000 USA

Copyright © 2010 by Gareth Stevens, Inc.

Executive Managing Editor: Lisa M. Herrington
Senior Editors: Barbara Bakowski, Jennifer Magid-Schiller
Designer: Jennifer Ryder-Talbot
Translators: Tatiana Acosta and Guillermo Gutiérrez

Photo Credits: Cover, back cover, title, pp. 15, 17, 21 © Ariel Skelley/Weekly Reader;
p. 7 © Katrina Brown/Shutterstock; p. 9 © Comstock/Jupiter Images; p. 11 © Jo Deluca/
Weekly Reader; p. 13 © Paula Cobleigh/Shutterstock; p. 19 © Ryan McVay/Getty Images

Printed in the United States of America

1 2 3 4 5 6 7 8 9 10 11 10 09

Table of Contents/Contenido

Boldface words appear in the glossary.
Las palabras en **negrita** aparecen en el glosario.

Welcome to November!

November is the 11th month of the year.

November has 30 days.

— — — — — — — — —

¡Bienvenidos a noviembre!

Noviembre es el undécimo mes del año.

Noviembre tiene 30 días.

Months of the Year/Meses del año

Month/Mes	Number of Days/ Días en el mes
1 January/Enero	31
2 February/Febrero	28 or 29*/28 ó 29*
3 March/Marzo	31
4 April/Abril	30
5 May/Mayo	31
6 June/Junio	30
7 July/Julio	31
8 August/Agosto	31
9 September/Septiembre	30
10 October/Octubre	31
11 **November/Noviembre**	**30**
12 December/Diciembre	31

*February has an extra day every fourth year./Febrero tiene un día extra cada cuatro años.

Fall Weather

November is a **fall** month. In some places, the weather turns cold.

- - - - - - - - -

Tiempo de otoño

Noviembre es uno de los meses del **otoño**. En algunos lugares, en noviembre empieza a hacer frío.

 What is the weather like in November where you live?

- - - - - - -

¿Qué tiempo hace en noviembre en el lugar donde vives?

Fall is **harvest** time. In November, the last of the fruits and vegetables are picked.

— — — — — — — — —

El otoño es época de **cosecha**. En noviembre se recogen las últimas frutas y verduras del año.

harvest/
cosecha

Special Days

Election Day occurs in early November. On this day, people choose their leaders by voting. Kids sometimes vote at school.

– – – – – – – – –

Días especiales

El **Día de las Elecciones** tiene lugar a comienzos de noviembre. Ese día, la gente vota para elegir a sus líderes. A veces, los niños participan en votaciones en las escuelas.

November 11 is **Veterans Day**.

It is a holiday to honor people who have served in the **armed forces**. Many veterans fought in wars to keep us safe and free.

— — — — — — — — — —

El 11 de noviembre es *Veterans Day* (Día de los Veteranos de Guerra). Ésta es una fiesta en honor a quienes han servido en las **fuerzas armadas**. Muchos veteranos han combatido en guerras para defender nuestra seguridad y libertad.

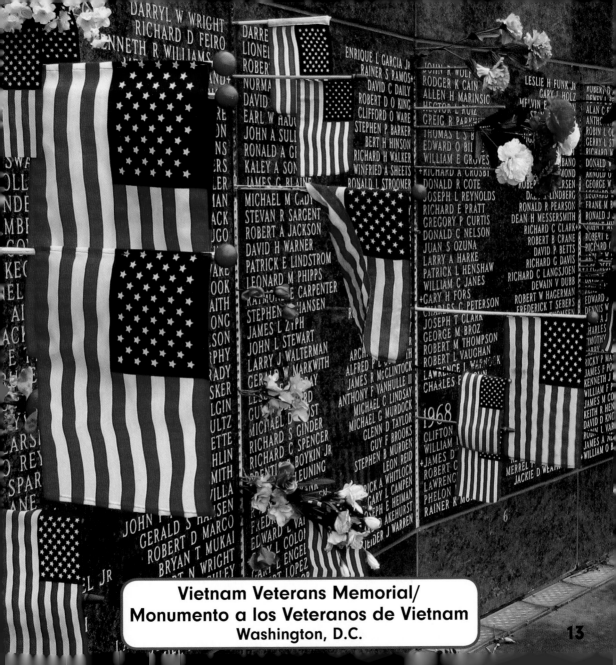

**Vietnam Veterans Memorial/
Monumento a los Veteranos de Vietnam**
Washington, D.C.

13

The fourth Thursday in November is Thanksgiving. People give thanks for the good things they have. They are thankful for special people in their lives.

— — — — — — — — —

El cuarto jueves de noviembre es el Día de Acción de Gracias. Ese día, agradecemos las cosas buenas que tenemos. Expresamos agradecimiento por estar rodeados de nuestros seres queridos.

People like to make special foods for Thanksgiving. They may cook turkey, potatoes, corn, and squash. Pie is a favorite dessert.

– – – – – – – – –

El Día de Acción de Gracias, muchas personas disfrutan cocinando platillos especiales. A veces preparan pavo, papas, maíz y calabaza. Los pasteles de frutas son uno de los postres preferidos ese día.

pie/pastel

17

Many people celebrate Thanksgiving by having a big dinner. They eat with family and friends.

– – – – – – – – –

Muchas personas celebran el Día de Acción de Gracias con una gran cena junto a sus parientes y amigos.

 What is your favorite food to eat on Thanksgiving?
¿Qué platillo típico del Día de Acción de Gracias es tu favorito?

When November ends, it is time
for December to begin. Soon it will
be winter.

— — — — — — — — — —

Cuando noviembre termina, empieza
diciembre. Pronto llegará el invierno.

Glossary/Glosario

armed forces: the army, navy, and other groups that defend a country

Election Day: a day to vote for public leaders, usually in early November

fall: the season between summer and winter, when the days get shorter and the weather gets cooler. It is also called autumn.

harvest: the fruits and vegetables gathered in a growing season

Veterans Day: a holiday to honor people who served in the armed forces

– – – – – – – – –

cosecha: frutas y verduras que se recogen al final de una temporada

Día de las Elecciones: día en que se vota para elegir a los cargos públicos

fuerzas armadas: el Ejército de Tierra, la Marina y otros grupos que se encargan de la defensa de una nación

otoño: la estación del año entre el verano y el invierno, en la que los días se acortan y el tiempo se vuelve más fresco

Veterans Day: fiesta en honor a las personas que han servido en las fuerzas armadas

For More Information/Más información

Books/Libros

How Corn Grows/Cómo crecen el maíz. How Plants Grow/
Cómo crecen las plantas (series). Joanne Mattern (Gareth
Stevens Publishing, 2006)

Thanksgiving/Día de Acción de Gracias. Our Country's
Holidays/Las fiestas de nuestra nación (series). Sheri Dean
(Gareth Stevens Publishing, 2006)

Web Sites/Páginas web

All About Thanksgiving/El Día de Acción de Gracias
www.kiddyhouse.com/Thanksgiving
Read the story of Thanksgiving./Conozcan la historia del
Día de Acción de Gracias.

Veterans Day Activities/Actividades para *Veterans Day*
www.apples4theteacher.com/holidays/veterans-day
Learn about the history of Veterans Day. Find coloring pages
and craft ideas, too./Conozcan la historia de *Veterans Day*.
Encuentren hojas para colorear y manualidades.

Index/Índice

About the Author

Robyn Brode has been a teacher, a writer, and an editor in the book publishing field for many years. She earned a bachelor's degree in English literature from the University of California, Berkeley.

Información sobre la autora

Robyn Brode ha sido maestra, escritora y editora de libros durante muchos años. Obtuvo su licenciatura en literatura inglesa en la Universidad de California, Berkeley.